The Unstoppable Eagles

Terri Lhuillier & Joanne Brady
Illustrated by Sarah Brady

Anderson, CA
USA

A Note From the Publisher

At the time of publication, due to the dedication of wildlife professionals over a period of 35 years, the bald eagle population has increased from a meager 417 nesting pairs to over 10,000 nesting pairs in the lower 48 states of the U.S.A. Bald eagles, once scarce in this region, have expanded their habitat to include urban areas. This behavioral adaptation opens new nesting territory to the eagle population.

At times, the overlap of human and eagle home ranges has caused concern and controversy. The story of Patriot and Liberty, of Redding, CA, holds many lessons as people continue *Working With Nature*™.

P.O. Box 1477
Anderson, CA 96007
www.redtail.com

find us on Facebook
facebook.com/TheUnstoppableEagles
facebook.com/RedTailPublishing

ISBN13: 978-0-9847756-2-0

Story © 2012 Terri Lhuillier & Joanne Brady
Illustrations © 2012 Sarah Brady
Critter Chit-Chatter™ © 2012 Red Tail Publishing. Educational contributions by Sharon Clay.
Critter Chit-Chatter™ and Working With Nature™ are trademarks of Red Tail Publishing.
Author/Illustrator photos and Critter Chit-Chatter™ Art by Mary A Livingston.
Story Editors: Jenny Main, Jillian Justice, Chris Livingston.

No Portion of this book or components may be reproduced or transmitted in any form or by any means, electronic or mechanical, including photocopying, recording, or by any informational storage and retrieval system available now or in the future, without the written permission from the publisher.

Two bald eagles flew high into the sky, soaring upon the rising thermals. Together, they performed a powerful sky dance filled with short chases, aerial loops, and breathtaking plunges. Declaring their courtship, they locked talons and cart-wheeled gracefully toward the earth.

Now that they found each other, it was time for the eagles to find a home.

Their search for a home ended in an ideal spot nestled in a stand of stately cottonwood trees. It was bordered by a rushing river and several tranquil ponds. These waterways were abundant with fish and waterfowl, their favorite foods.

This was a perfect place for an eagle's home.

As fall drew near, the eagles began the task of nest building. They chose a tall cottonwood tree that could support the weight of their massive nest. Breaking off branches, the eagles carried them to a fork in the tree. With their beaks, they carefully wove each stick into place forming a large, bowl-shaped aerie, nearly 100 feet off the ground.

Below the nest was a bustling highway bridge. Commuters, shoppers, and visitors crossed it daily while traveling in and about the city.

    As the eagle population grew from year to year, so did the population of the city. The overcrowded bridge could no longer support the number of drivers crossing it each day.

    Engineers surveyed for a new and wider bridge. The construction would last for years and cause a great deal of clatter and commotion near the eagles' home.

As temperatures grew colder and daylight grew shorter, the bald eagles spent their days guarding their nesting territory. Together they teamed up to chase off hawks, vultures, and other intruders.

Once the last of the golden cottonwood leaves fell to the ground, the eagles' nest became easily visible. Local bird watchers spotted the large mass of sticks in the barren tree and knew it must belong to the bald eagle pair.

When the bridge builders saw how close the eagles' nest was to the highway bridge, they grew concerned. Fearing the eagles might abandon their eggs or eaglets, as other eagles have done when disturbed, they contacted wildlife officials.

The wildlife experts decided the best plan was to **stop the eagles** from nesting near the bridge construction. They hoped by blocking the nest, the eagles would move to a safer location.

Following the wildlife experts' orders, the bridge builders built a plastic cone large enough to cover the eagles' nest. As one climber worked his way up the tall cottonwood, a second climber attached the cone to a chain and pulley. It was raised up the length of the tree and placed on top of the nest. The tree climbers secured the cone and descended quickly to the ground.

After spending the day hunting along the river, the eagles followed each other toward the nest tree. Approaching their home, they spotted an unusual object.

A **huge, black cone** was sitting right on top of their nest!

The eagles fiercely defended their home. With talons outstretched, they took turns swooping and diving at the strange intruder. They tried chasing the cone away, as they had done when hawks, turkey vultures, and other trespassers dared to venture too close. However, this unusual object was behaving differently. Despite their efforts, the eagle pair could not force the stubborn invader to leave.

Bird watchers below noticed the commotion above. They were appalled and wondered why a cone had been placed on top of the eagles' nest.

Word spread and concern grew. The courage and tenacity displayed by the eagles inspired the community to take action. They searched for another way to keep the eagles safe.

As for the eagles, instead of leaving, they set about building a new nest. They gathered branches and carried them one by one to a neighboring cottonwood tree.

The eagles' new nest was just starting to take shape, when suddenly, a strange trespasser entered their territory! It was a two-legged intruder wearing a bright, red helmet. Up the tree he came. The eagles watched while their nest came under attack. One by one, the tree climber tossed each of the carefully placed sticks to the ground until no sign of the eagles' new home remained.

The news spread quickly. People were outraged. Many believed there had to be another way to protect the eagles during construction. The people rallied together to come up with a better plan, one that would allow the eagles to stay.

The people met with the bridge builders. Everyone was anxious knowing the fate of the eagle pair was about to be decided. As they introduced themselves, personal stories of love, respect, and admiration for the bald eagle were shared.

Awaiting the decision, faces grew solemn, tears welled, and the room fell silent.

A bridge builder rose and addressed the crowd, "Since these determined eagles are showing no intention of leaving, we want you to know the cone is coming down tomorrow!"

The room erupted with cheers of joy and relief!

The next day everyone gathered near the nest site. Excitement filled the air as the crowd watched a tree climber in a red helmet scale the cottonwood tree. He unchained the cone that had been blocking the eagles from their nest for thirty-two days. The cone was lowered to the ground, freeing the eagles' home at last!

Onlookers hugged and cheered. They scanned the sky hoping to spot the eagles. Minutes became hours, with no sign of the eagles. Fearing it was too little too late, the disheartened crowd slowly dispersed.

   As the sun settled behind the surrounding foothills, the two eagles quietly returned home.

   Cautiously, the female eagle entered her unblocked nest while the male eagle watched and waited. Within minutes, he joined his mate and the two eagles instinctively began rearranging sticks, pulling up soft material, and preparing the nest bowl for egg laying.

   Word of their return spread quickly. Not only had they won back their nest, they had also won the hearts of the townspeople.

Embracing them as members of the community, the people wanted to choose names for the two eagles. A contest was held and once the votes were counted, the male was given the name, *Patriot*, and the female, *Liberty*.

Two months passed and with steady rain dampening the nest, Liberty laid her first egg. Three days later, with Patriot by her side, she laid a second.

Below the nest, construction crews worked day and night while the eagles took shifts incubating their eggs. Over the next thirty-five days, the pair sheltered them from cold, wind, and rain. Every few hours, they gently nudged and rolled the fragile eggs to ensure even heating.

A wildlife biologist continuously monitored the eagles as pile drivers pounded, dust flew, and workers scurried. Despite the deafening noise and constant commotion, the eagle pair remained.

In early spring, while the nest tree swayed gently in the warm breeze, the first eaglet began to hatch. The chick cracked a small opening in the solid shell using the egg tooth on top of its beak and gradually worked its way out. Three days later, a second gray, fuzzy chick emerged. Liberty kept them tucked safely beneath her while Patriot searched the nearby river and ponds for food.

Bird watchers admired the dedication of the eagles as they kept their young well-fed and sheltered. Patriot and Liberty snatched fish and waterfowl several times a day for their rapidly growing chicks. They tore off bite-sized fragments and placed them tenderly in the eaglets' wide, open beaks.

Commuters passing through the construction zone were often treated to up close sightings of Patriot and Liberty with a fish dangling from their talons. Construction workers also grew accustomed to the famous eagle pair flying to and from the nest.

At ten weeks old, the eaglets spent their days flapping and exercising their enormous wings. Gaining confidence, they took short jumps from the nest to branches in the tall cottonwood tree.

Two weeks later, with wings fully developed the fledglings were ready to take their first flight. Following their parents' lead, the two young eagles leaped upward, flapped forcefully, and dove bravely out of the nest.

Patriot and Liberty called loudly with beaks raised while watching their eaglets soar freely above the highway bridge. The young eagles had no idea what their parents had gone through to raise them amongst the clamor and commotion of city life.

In the end, everyone realized something Patriot and Liberty had known from the very beginning…this was a perfect place for an eagle's home.

Critter Chit-Chatter™

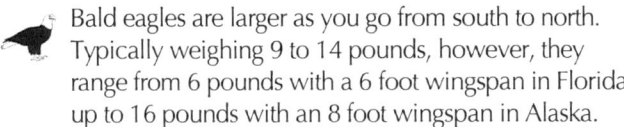

Bald Eagle

GLOSSARY OF TERMS:

aerie - an eagle's nest

branching - when the eaglets begin to hop to the branches around the nest; the step just prior to fledging

DDT - dichlorodiphenyltrichloroethane is a pesticide used in the 1940s that caused many birds to lay eggs with thin shells; banned by the U.S.A. in 1972

dimorphic - having two distinct forms

egg cup - an indentation in the nest lined with soft grasses where the eggs are laid, also called **nest bowl**

egg tooth - a hard bump on the tip of a chick's beak used to break through the eggshell at hatching, a physical adaptation

Endangered Species List - a federal law adopted in 1973 to protect plants and animals in danger of becoming extinct

engineer - a person trained in design and construction

Environmental Assessment (EA) - a scientific study of the environment as it relates to activities

Environmental Impact Report (EIR) - a scientific document that addresses the impact of activities on the environment

fledgling - a young bird old enough to make its first full flight away from the nest

incubation - the amount of time from when an egg is laid until it hatches

raptor - a bird of prey including eagles, hawks and falcons

stand - a group of trees

survey - to view or examine detail

talons - a raptor's claws

wildlife biologist - a person who is a specialist in the study of wildlife

For more information on bald eagles:

Cornell lab of Ornithology - www.allaboutbirds.org

The American Eagle Foundation - www.eagles.org

- Scientific name: Halieaeetus leucocephalus, means "the white headed fisherman."

- Bald eagles are larger as you go from south to north. Typically weighing 9 to 14 pounds, however, they range from 6 pounds with a 6 foot wingspan in Florida up to 16 pounds with an 8 foot wingspan in Alaska.

- Male and female bald eagles are not sexually dimorphic. Males and females look the same. However, females are about 1/3 larger than males.

- Bald eagles use the same nest each year, adding to it until it becomes massive. In 2010, the largest bald eagle nest was located near Cape Canaveral, Florida. It was 10 feet wide and 20 feet deep, weighing an estimated 3 tons!

- They typically lay 2 eggs the size of goose eggs. Incubation is on average 35 days.

- When eaglets fledge they often appear larger than the parents because their flight feathers and tail feathers are slightly longer. This gives them more stability while they are mastering flying and hunting.

- Eagles do not get their white head and tail until they are between 3-5 years of age.

- Their feet are very strong and have small hooks on the bottoms to hold onto fish.

- Bald eagles eat mainly fish. They also eat small mammals, coots and carrion.

- Some bald eagles migrate while others stay in the area year-round. Patriot and Liberty do not migrate.

- The bald eagle is only found in North America and is the national symbol of the United States.

- DDT and shootings brought the bald eagle population down to a low of about 417 nesting pairs in the lower 48 states and were listed endangered in 1976.

- With the help of captive breeding programs and new laws, the bald eagle population increased to about 10,000 pairs and were removed from the Endangered Species List 2007.

- The use of a plastic cone is a common, acceptable exclusion method used for years. Birds see the nest us unavailable and find another nesting site.

- Bald eagles mate for life only choosing another if their mate should die.